COMFORT
OF THE AFFLICTED

DEVOTION TO MARY

With Ecclesiastical Approval

© 2015 Chintamani Books
New York, New York
All rights reserved.

ISBN 978-0-9960236-9-6

TABLE OF CONTENTS

BLESSED MOTHER'S WORDS

Magnificat	*11*
Mother of Mercy	*12*
Our Lady of Guadalupe	*14*
Daily Prayer	*15*
Our Lady of Fatima	*17*

ROSARY PRAYERS

Crown of Roses	*21*
Benefits of Praying the Rosary	*23*
The Blessings of the Rosary	*23*
The Fifteen Promises	
of the Blessed Virgin Mary	*25*
How to Pray the Rosary	*28*
Rosary Prayers	*30*
The Joyful Mysteries	*34*
The Luminous Mysteries	*38*
The Sorrowful Mysteries	*42*
The Glorious Mysteries	*46*

SEVEN SORROWS OF MARY

Seven Sorrows of Mary	53
The Seven Graces	
* promised by the Blessed Mother*	54
Devotion to the Seven Sorrows of Mary	56
How to Pray the Rosary	
* of the Seven Sorrows of Mary*	57
The Seven Sorrows of Mary	61

LITANIES & NOVENAS

Litany of Loreto	69
Litany of the Blessed Virgin Mary	75
Novena to the Blessed Virgin Mary	80
Litany of the Immaculate Heart of Mary	83
Novena to the Immaculate Heart of Mary	87
Novena Prayer	
* to the Immaculate Heart of Mary*	94
Miraculous Medal Novena	95

CONSECRATIONS & REPARATIONS

Consecration	
* to the Most Blessed and Sweet Virgin Mary*	103

Consecration for Victory against Temptations	106
Official Act of Consecration	107
Act of Reparation for Insults	109
Act of Reparation for Blasphemy	110
Act of Reparation to the Immaculate Heart of Mary	112
Act of Reparation through the Blessed Virgin Mary	114
Prayer for Reunion	116
Prayer	118
Divine Praises	120

DEVOTIONAL PRAYERS

Psalm 45:9-17	123
Under Your Protection	125
Hail, You Star of the Ocean	126
Loving Mother of Our Redeemer	128
The Angel	129
Remember	131
Hail Queen of Heaven	132
Queen of Heaven	133
Hail Holy Queen	134

SELECTED LATIN PRAYERS

Rosarium	*137*
Litaniae Lauretanae	*140*
Novena ad Beatam Mariam Virginem	*146*
Sub Tuum Praesidium	*149*
Ave Maris Stella	*150*
Alma Redemptoris Mater	*152*
Angelus	*153*
Memorare	*155*
Ave Regina Caelorum	*156*
Regina Caeli	*157*
Salve Regina	*158*

CONTEMPORARY DEVOTIONS

Heavenly Queen	*161*
Luminous Pearl	*164*
Rose of Morning Rising	*165*
Radiant Mercy	*166*
Clement Mother	*168*
Evening Prayer	*169*
Chimes	*170*
Nativity	*171*
Gate of Heaven	*172*

BLESSED MOTHER'S

WORDS

MAGNIFICAT

My soul glorifies the Lord. My spirit rejoices in God my Savior, for He smiles upon the humility of His servant. From this time forward, all generations will call me blessed. The Almighty works marvels for me—Holy is His name. His mercy extends from generation to generation, for those in awe of Him. He puts forth His arm in strength and scatters the proud-hearted. He casts the mighty from their thrones and uplifts the humble. He fills the hungry with good things but sends the rich away empty. He protects His servant Israel, remembering His mercy, as promised to Abraham and his descendants, forever.

The Blessed Mother spoke these words when she visited her cousin Elizabeth. They are now known as the Magnificat.
Luke 1:46-55

MOTHER OF MERCY

I, WHO SPEAK TO YOU, am the Queen of Heaven. I am like a gardener of this world. When a gardener sees the rise of strong wind, harmful to the little plants and the trees of his garden, at once he runs to them, binding them fast to sturdy stakes as best he can. He comes to their aid in various ways, according to his ability, lest they be broken by the rushing wind or be wretchedly uprooted.

I, the Mother of Mercy, do the same in the garden of this world. When I see the dangerous winds of temptations and wicked suggestions blowing on people's hearts, at once I have recourse to my Lord and my God, my Son Jesus Christ. I pray and obtain from my Son the outpouring of the Holy Spirit into their hearts, to prop them up and savingly confirm them, that they may continue spiritually uninjured by the diabolic wind of temptations, lest evil prevail against mankind, breaking souls and plucking them up by the stem in accordance with unholy desires.

When people receive, with humility of heart and active compliance, these said stakes of mine and my assistance, at once they are defended against the infernal onslaught of temptations. Remaining firm in the state of grace, they bear for God and for me the fruit of sweetness in due season.

The Blessed Mother appeared to Saint Bridget (451-523) and spoke these words.

OUR LADY OF GUADALUPE

I TRULY AM your merciful Mother, your Mother and the Mother of all who dwell in this land, and of all mankind, of all those who love me, of those who cry to me, and of those who seek and place their trust in me.

Here, I shall listen to your weeping and sorrows. I shall hold you all to my heart, and I shall cure many sufferings, afflictions, and sorrows.

The Blessed Mother appeared to Saint Juan Diego at the Hill of Tepeyac on December 9, 1531 and spoke these words.

DAILY PRAYER

I prostrate myself in your presence, O God Most High, and I give you thanks and praise for your Immutable Being, for your Infinite Perfections, and for having created me out of nothing.

I acknowledge myself as your creature and as the work of your hands. I bless you, and I adore you. I give you honor, magnificence, and divinity as the Supreme Lord and Creator of myself and of all that exists.

I raise up my spirit to place it into your hands. I offer myself with profound humility and resignation to you, and I ask you to dispose of me according to your Holy Will, during this day and during all the days of my life. I ask you to teach me to fulfill whatever would be to your greater pleasure.

I consult you, I ask your advice, I ask your permission, and I ask your blessing on everything that I do today.

I ask your permission to use my body as your temple, my mind as the mind of Christ, my soul as the souls of Jesus and Mary, my memory to remember only you, my will to use in conformity to your will, and my understanding to understand you with your wisdom and to understand my brothers and sisters.

The Virgin Mary appeared to Sister Mary of Agreda (1602-1665) and offered these words to be used as daily prayer.

OUR LADY OF FATIMA

Pray the rosary every day to obtain peace for the world…Many souls will be saved, and there will be peace.

Pray, pray a great deal, and make sacrifices for sinners. So many souls go to hell, because there is no one to pray and sacrifice for them.

Do you suffer a great deal? Don't be discouraged. I will never abandon you. My Immaculate Heart will be your refuge, and through it you will find God… In the end, my Immaculate Heart will triumph.

Our Lady of Fatima appeared at Cova de Iria six times between 1916 and 1917. She appeared to the children Lucia Dos Santos and her cousins Francisco and Jacinta Marto in a meadow, while they pastured sheep and prayed the Rosary. She spoke these words to the children.

THE ROSARY

(ROSARIUM)

CROWN OF ROSES

Prayer and kind deeds bloom as flowers in the Blessed Mother's heavenly garden. Our tears of repentance and acts of conversion water this garden. To pray the Rosary is to select each most beautiful rose, queen of all flowers, to weave them into a garland, and to crown her. The word rosary means "Crown of Roses."

Praying the Rosary cultivates the garden of our hearts as well, that the Blessed Mother's garden may bloom on earth as it does in heaven.

With each divine Mystery we pray, the Blessed Mother offers us a virtue upon which to meditate. These virtues are her virtues, and those of Our Lord. In meditating upon these virtues, we learn from the life of the Blessed Mother and Our Lord, that we may emulate what they contain and realize what they promise. As we hold each fruit of the divine Mystery in quiet contemplation, the virtue ripens in our hearts.

So, our hearts become fragrant with prayerful flower and fruit to be offered to the Blessed Mother.

The Blessed Mother bestowed the grace of the Rosary, with its Joyful Mysteries, Sorrowful

Mysteries, and Glorious Mysteries, upon us in 1214. She appeared to Saint Dominic and revealed the Rosary prayers as a powerful means of conversion from a life of sin to one of virtue. Later, in 2002, Saint Pope John Paul II sanctified the Luminous Mysteries.

To pray the Rosary is a complete experience that embraces all that is here in this world and beyond. The Rosary prayers celebrate joy, light, and glory, and also sorrow, as a part of life.

Indeed, grief is a mystical experience to be reverenced, that the sorrows may open us more deeply to the presence of the Blessed Mother and Our Lord. We need not turn from worldly woes but hold them with faith and love in the light of the heart, as children of the Blessed Mother, that we may one day awaken to the transcendent glory of Our Lord.

The Blessed Mother asks us to pray the Rosary daily that there may be peace on earth.

COMFORT OF THE AFFLICTED

Benefits of Praying the Rosary

1. Praying the Rosary gradually awakens perfect wisdom, the knowledge of Jesus Christ.

2. Praying the Rosary purifies our souls, cleansing us of sin.

3. Praying the Rosary brings victory over our enemies, those external and internal (ie. sinful tendencies).

4. Praying the Rosary makes it easy for us to practice virtue.

5. Praying the Rosary lights the heart's sacred fire with love for Our Lord.

6. Praying the Rosary blesses us with graces and merits.

7. Praying the Rosary supplies us with what we need to pay our debts to God and to all of mankind; and finally, it obtains countless graces for us from Almighty God.

COMFORT OF THE AFFLICTED

The Blessings of the Rosary

1. Sinners are forgiven.

2. Souls that thirst are refreshed.

3. Those fettered have their bonds broken.

4. Those who weep are renewed in joy.

5. Those who are tempted find salvation.

6. The poor receive sustenance.

7. The religious are reformed.

8. The ignorant are instructed.

9. The living surrender pride for humility.

10. The dead have their pains eased by prayerful intercession.

THE FIFTEEN PROMISES
OF THE BLESSED VIRGIN MARY

1. Whoever shall faithfully serve me by the recitation of the Rosary shall receive signal graces.

2. I promise my special protection and the greatest graces to all those who recite the Rosary.

3. The Rosary shall be a powerful armor against hell. It will destroy vice, decrease sin, and defeat heresies.

4. The Rosary shall cause virtue and good works to flourish. It will obtain for souls the abundant mercy of God. It will withdraw the hearts of people from the love of the world and its vanities, and will lift them to the desire of eternal things. O, that souls would sanctify themselves by this means.

5. The soul which recommends itself to me by the recitation of the Rosary shall not perish.

6. Those who recite the Rosary devoutly, contemplating its sacred Mysteries, shall never be conquered by misfortune. God will not chastise such souls in His justice, nor shall they perish without provision for death. If souls be just, they shall remain in the grace of God and become worthy of eternal life.

7. Whoever has true devotion for the Rosary will not die without the Sacraments of the Church.

8. Those who faithfully recite the Rosary shall have, during their life and at their death, the light of God and the plentitude of His graces. At the moment of death, they shall participate in the merits of the saints in paradise.

9. I shall deliver from purgatory those who have been devoted to the Rosary.

10. The faithful children of the Rosary shall merit a high degree of glory in heaven.

11. You shall obtain all that you ask of me by the recitation of the Rosary.

12. All those who propagate the holy Rosary shall be aided by me in their necessities.

13. I have obtained from my divine Son the favor that all advocates of the Rosary shall have for intercessors the entire celestial court during their life and at the hour of death.

14. All who recite the Rosary are my children, brothers and sisters of my only Son, Jesus Christ.

15. Devotion to my Rosary is a great sign of predestination.

How to Pray the Rosary

1. Holding the crucifix, make the Sign of the Cross. Then, recite the Apostles' Creed.

2. On the first large bead, recite the Our Father.

3. On each of the three small beads, recite a Hail Mary, for an increase in faith, hope, and charity.

4. On the next large bead, recite the Glory Be to the Father.

5. Recall the first Rosary Mystery of the day, and on the next large bead, recite the Our Father.

MONDAY: Joyful Mysteries
TUESDAY: Sorrowful Mysteries
WEDNESDAY: Glorious Mysteries
THURSDAY: Luminous Mysteries
FRIDAY: Sorrowful Mysteries
SATURDAY: Joyful Mysteries
SUNDAY: Glorious Mysteries

NOTE: The Joyful Mysteries are meditated upon on Sundays of Advent and Sundays between Epiphany

COMFORT OF THE AFFLICTED

and Lent. The Sorrowful Mysteries are meditated upon on Sundays during Lent.

6. On each of the ten small beads to follow, recite a Hail Mary, while reflecting on the relevant Mystery. These ten Angelic Salutations are also referred to as a decade.

7. On the next large bead, recite the Glory Be to the Father to close out the decade. Then, recite the Our Father to begin a new decade.

8. Each succeeding decade is prayed in a similar manner, by contemplating the relevant Mystery and then praying the Our Father, ten Hail Marys, and the Glory Be to the Father.

9. After each decade, pray the Fatima Prayer (Almighty Jesus).

10. When the fifth Mystery has been prayed, conclude with the Hail Holy Queen.

COMFORT OF THE AFFLICTED

ROSARY PRAYERS

MAKE THE SIGN + OF THE CROSS (SIGNUM CRUCIS)

In the name of the Father, the Son, and the Holy Spirit. Amen.

PRAY THE APOSTLES' CREED (CREDO)

I believe in God, the Father Almighty, Creator of Heaven and Earth. I believe in Jesus Christ, His only Son, our Lord. He was conceived by the power of the Holy Spirit and born of the Virgin Mary. He suffered under Pontius Pilate, was crucified, died, and was buried. On the third day, He rose again. He ascended into heaven and is seated at the right hand of the Father. He will come again in glory to judge the living and the dead. I believe in the Holy Spirit, the holy catholic Church, the communion of saints, the forgiveness of sins, the resurrection of the dead, and life everlasting. Amen.

COMFORT OF THE AFFLICTED

Pray the Our Father (Pater Noster)

Our Father who lives in heaven, hallowed be your name. Your kingdom come, your will be done, on earth as it is in heaven. Give us this day our daily bread, and forgive us our trespasses, as we forgive those who trespass against us, and lead us not into temptation, but deliver us from evil. Amen.

Pray three Hail Marys (Ave Maria)

Hail Mary, full of grace, the Lord is with you. Blessed are you among women, and blessed is the fruit of your womb, Jesus. Holy Mary, Mother of God, pray for us sinners, now and at the hour of our death. Amen.

Pray the Glory Be to the Father (Gloria Patri)

Glory be to the Father, to the Son, and to the Holy Spirit. As it was in the beginning, so it is now, and ever shall be—world without end. Amen.

COMFORT OF THE AFFLICTED

Pray the Five Mysteries (the Our Father, ten Hail Marys, the Glory Be to the Father, and the Fatima Prayer for each Mystery)

Pray the Fatima Prayer (Oratio Fatimae)

Almighty Jesus, forgive us our sins. Save us from the fires of Hell. Lead all souls to heaven, especially those most in need of your mercy.

Pray the Hail Holy Queen (Salve Regina)

Hail, Holy Queen, Mother of Mercy, our life, our sweetness, and our hope. To you do we cry, poor banished children of Eve. To you do we send up our sighs, mourning, and weeping in this valley of tears. Turn then, most gracious advocate, your eyes of mercy toward us, and after this, our exile, show unto us the blessed fruit of your womb, Jesus. O clement, O loving, O sweet Virgin Mary.

Pray for us, O holy Mother of God, that we may be made worthy of the promises of Christ. Amen.

COMFORT OF THE AFFLICTED

PRAYER AFTER THE ROSARY

O God, whose only-begotten Son, by His life, death, and resurrection, has purchased for us the rewards of eternal life; grant, we beseech you, that we who meditate upon these mysteries of the most holy Rosary of the Blessed Virgin Mary, may imitate what they contain and obtain what they promise. We ask this through Christ our Lord. Amen.

COMFORT OF THE AFFLICTED

The Joyful Mysteries

The Joyful Mysteries are prayed on Mondays and Saturdays. They are optional on Sundays during Advent and the Christmas Season.

First Mystery: Annunciation

The angel appeared to Mary and said, "Hail, full of grace, the Lord is with you. Blessed are you among women." Mary was troubled, but the angel said, "Fear not, for you have found favor with the Lord. Behold, you will conceive and bear a son, and you shall call him Jesus."

Luke 1:28-31

Fruit of the Mystery: Humility

Pray the Our Father.
Pray ten Hail Marys.
Pray the Glory Be to the Father.
Pray the Fatima Prayer.

COMFORT OF THE AFFLICTED

SECOND MYSTERY: VISITATION

When Elizabeth heard Mary's salutation, the babe leapt in her womb, and Elizabeth was filled with the Holy Spirit. She cried out in a loud voice, "Blessed are you among women, and blessed is the fruit of your womb."

Luke 1:41-42

FRUIT OF THE MYSTERY: LOVE OF NEIGHBOR

Pray the Our Father.
Pray ten Hail Marys.
Pray the Glory Be to the Father.
Pray the Fatima Prayer.

THIRD MYSTERY: NATIVITY

Mary brought forth her first-born son. She wrapped him in swaddling clothes and laid him in a manger, because there was no room for them at the inn. In the same country were shepherds abiding in the field, keeping watch over their flock by night. Lo, the angel of the Lord appeared. The glory of the Lord shone all around them, and they were afraid. The angel said, "Fear not. Behold, I bring good tidings of great joy for all people. This day, in the city of David, is born a savior, Christ the Lord."

Luke 2:7-11

COMFORT OF THE AFFLICTED

Fruit of the Mystery: Poverty

Pray the Our Father.
Pray ten Hail Marys.
Pray the Glory Be to the Father.
Pray the Fatima Prayer.

Fourth Mystery: Presentation

When the days of Mary's purification according to the law of Moses were accomplished, Mary and Joseph brought the child to Jerusalem to present him to the Lord, for it is written in the law of the Lord, "Every male that opens the womb shall be consecrated to the Lord."

Luke 2:22-23

Fruit of the Mystery: Obedience

Pray the Our Father.
Pray ten Hail Marys.
Pray the Glory Be to the Father.
Pray the Fatima Prayer.

COMFORT OF THE AFFLICTED

FIFTH MYSTERY: FINDING THE CHILD

After three days, Mary and Joseph found Jesus in the temple, sitting amidst the teachers, listening and asking them questions. All who heard him were amazed at his understanding and responses.

Luke 2:46-47

FRUIT OF THE MYSTERY: JOY IN SALVATION

Pray the Our Father.
Pray ten Hail Marys.
Pray the Glory Be to the Father.
Pray the Fatima Prayer.

The Luminous Mysteries

The Luminous Mysteries are prayed on Thursdays.

First Mystery: Baptism

Jesus came from Nazareth of Galilee and was baptized by John in the Jordan River. Straightway, coming up out of the water, he saw the heavens opened and the Spirit like a dove descending upon him. A voice came from heaven saying, "You are my beloved Son, in whom I am well pleased."

Mark 1:9-11

Fruit of the Mystery: Opening to the Holy Spirit

Pray the Our Father.
Pray ten Hail Marys.
Pray the Glory Be to the Father.
Pray the Fatima Prayer.

COMFORT OF THE AFFLICTED

Second Mystery: Wedding Feast at Cana

His mother said to the servants, "Do whatever he tells you to do." Six stone waterpots were set out, each to hold nearly twenty-seven gallons. Jesus said to them, "Fill the waterpots with water," and the servants filled them up to the brim. The ruler of the feast tasted the water that was made wine and knew not how this had happened, but the servants who had drawn the water knew.

John 2:5-9

Fruit of the Mystery: To Jesus through Mary

Pray the Our Father.
Pray ten Hail Marys.
Pray the Glory Be to the Father.
Pray the Fatima Prayer.

Third Mystery: Proclaming the Kingdom

After John the Baptist was imprisoned, Jesus came into Galilee, preaching the gospel of the kingdom of God. He said, "The time is fulfilled, and the kingdom of God is at hand. Repent, and believe."

Mark 1:14-15

COMFORT OF THE AFFLICTED

FRUIT OF THE MYSTERY: REPENTANCE AND CONVERSION

Pray the Our Father.
Pray ten Hail Marys.
Pray the Glory Be to the Father.
Pray the Fatima Prayer.

FOURTH MYSTERY: TRANSFIGURATION

After six days, Jesus took Peter, James, and John up into a high mountain, and was transfigured before them. His face shone like the sun, and his raiment was white with light. Behold, there appeared Moses and Elijah talking with him…A bright cloud appeared, and a voice from the cloud said, "This is my beloved Son, in whom I am well pleased. Listen to him."

Matthew 17:1-5

FRUIT OF THE MYSTERY: LONGING FOR HOLINESS

Pray the Our Father.
Pray ten Hail Marys.
Pray the Glory Be to the Father.
Pray the Fatima Prayer.

COMFORT OF THE AFFLICTED

Fifth Mystery: Institution of the Eucharist

Jesus said to the disciples, "I longed to eat this Passover supper with you before the suffering begins."...He took bread and gave thanks, and broke it and gave it to them, saying, "This is my body, which is to be given up for you. Do this in memory of me." Likewise, he offered the cup after supper, saying, "This cup is the new covenant in my blood, which is to be shed for you."

Luke 22:15-20

Fruit of the Mystery: Adoration

Pray the Our Father.
Pray ten Hail Marys.
Pray the Glory Be to the Father.
Pray the Fatima Prayer.

The Sorrowful Mysteries

The Sorrowful Mysteries are prayed on Tuesdays and Fridays. They are optional on Sundays during Lent.

First Mystery: Agony in the Garden

Jesus went, as he often did, to the Mount of Olives, and his disciples followed him. He said to them, "Pray that you do not enter into temptation." Then, he withdrew, knelt, and prayed saying, "Father, if you are willing, let this cup pass from me; nevertheless, let not my will but your will be done." An angel appeared from heaven and strengthened him. In agony, he prayed more earnestly, and his sweat was like drops of blood falling to the ground.

Luke 22:39-44

Fruit of the Mystery: Sorrow for Sin

Pray the Our Father.
Pray ten Hail Marys.
Pray the Glory Be to the Father.
Pray the Fatima Prayer.

COMFORT OF THE AFFLICTED

S ECOND M YSTERY: S COURGING

Pilate went out again to the Jews and said to them, "I find no fault in him at all, but you have a custom—that I should release one imprisoned to you at the Passover. Would you like me to release the King of the Jews?" They all cried out saying, "Not this man but Barabbas." (Barabbas was a robber.) Therefore, Pilate took Jesus and scourged him."

John 18:38-40, 19:1

F RUIT OF THE M YSTERY: P URITY

Pray the Our Father.
Pray ten Hail Marys.
Pray the Glory Be to the Father.
Pray the Fatima Prayer.

T HIRD M YSTERY: C ROWNING WITH T HORNS

Pilate's soldiers took Jesus into the common hall and gathered a band of soldiers around him. They stripped him and wrapped him in a scarlet robe. When they had woven a crown of thorns, they placed it on his head and stuck a reed in his right hand. Then, they knelt before him and mocked him saying, "Hail, King of the Jews." They spat upon him and took the reed and smote his head.

Matthew 27:27-30

COMFORT OF THE AFFLICTED

FRUIT OF THE MYSTERY: COURAGE

Pray the Our Father.
Pray ten Hail Marys.
Pray the Glory Be to the Father.
Pray the Fatima Prayer.

FOURTH MYSTERY: CARRYING THE CROSS

They led Jesus away and laid hold of Simon, a Cyrenian farmer, to help Jesus carry the cross. A great crowd and a group of women, who wailed and lamented him, followed. Jesus turned to the women and said, "Daughters of Jerusalem, weep not for me, but weep for yourselves, and for your children."

Luke 23:26-29

FRUIT OF THE MYSTERY: PATIENCE

Pray the Our Father.
Pray ten Hail Marys.
Pray the Glory Be to the Father.
Pray the Fatima Prayer.

COMFORT OF THE AFFLICTED

Fifth Mystery: Crucifixion

When they reached the place called Calvary, they crucified Jesus and the criminals, one at his right hand and the other at his left. Then, Jesus said, "Father, forgive them, for they know not what they do." The people watched. The rulers derided him saying, "He saved others. Let him save himself, if he be the Christ, the chosen of God." The soldiers mocked him and offered him vinegar to drink... One of the criminals said to Jesus, "Lord, remember me when you come into your kingdom." Jesus said to him, "Today, you shall be with me in paradise." For three hours, darkness fell upon the earth. The sun was darkened, and the veil of the temple was torn. Jesus cried out in a loud voice and said, "Father, into your hands I commend my spirit." Having said this, he expired.

Luke 33:35-46

Fruit of the Mystery: Perseverance

Pray the Our Father.
Pray ten Hail Marys.
Pray the Glory Be to the Father.
Pray the Fatima Prayer.

The Glorious Mysteries

The Glorious Mysteries are prayed on Wednesdays and Sundays.

First Mystery: Resurrection

There was a great earthquake, for the angel of the Lord descended from heaven, rolled the stone from the door of the tomb, and sat upon it. His countenance was like lightning, and his raiment white as snow. In fear, the keepers shook and became like dead men. The angel said to the women, "Fear not. I know that you seek Jesus who was crucified. He is not here, for he is risen, as he foretold. Come, see the place where the Lord lay. Go quickly, and tell the disciples that he is risen from the dead. Behold, he has gone into Galilee. There, you will see him."

Matthew 28:2-7

Fruit of the Mystery: Faith

Pray the Our Father.
Pray ten Hail Marys.
Pray the Glory Be to the Father.
Pray the Fatima Prayer.

COMFORT OF THE AFFLICTED

SECOND MYSTERY: ASCENSION

He appeared to the eleven disciples as they sat and ate, and he upbraided them for their disbelief and hardness of heart, because they had not believed those who had seen him after he had risen. Then, he said to them, "Go throughout the world, and preach the good news to every creature."...After the Lord spoke to the disciples, he was received into heaven and sat at the right hand of God.
Mark 16:14-19

FRUIT OF THE MYSTERY: HOPE

Pray the Our Father.
Pray ten Hail Marys.
Pray the Glory Be to the Father.
Pray the Fatima Prayer.

THIRD MYSTERY: DESCENT OF THE HOLY SPIRIT

When the day of Pentecost arrived, the disciples were of one accord and in one place. Suddenly, from heaven came the sound of a rushing mighty wind. It filled the house where they sat. There appeared to them cloven tongues of fire that sat upon each of them. They were filled with the Holy Spirit and began to speak with other tongues, as the Spirit gave them utterance. Dwelling in Jerusalem were

COMFORT OF THE AFFLICTED

Jews, devout men from every nation under heaven. The multitude came together and were confounded, because every man heard the disciples speak in his own language.
Acts 2:1-6

FRUIT OF THE MYSTERY: LOVE FOR THE LORD

Pray the Our Father.
Pray ten Hail Marys.
Pray the Glory Be to the Father.
Pray the Fatima Prayer.

FOURTH MYSTERY: ASSUMPTION OF THE VIRGIN

My dove, my undefiled, is but one. She is the only one of her mother. She is the choice one of she who bore her. The daughters saw her and blessed her. The queens and the concubines, they praised her. Who is she that rises like the dawn, fair as the moon, bright as the sun, and terrible as an army in battle array?"
Song of Solomon 6:9-10

FRUIT OF THE MYSTERY: GRACE OF A HAPPY DEATH

Pray the Our Father.
Pray ten Hail Marys.
Pray the Glory Be to the Father.
Pray the Fatima Prayer.

COMFORT OF THE AFFLICTED

FIFTH MYSTERY: CORONATION OF THE VIRGIN

The temple of God was opened in heaven. In the temple was seen the ark of His covenant. There were lightnings, voices, thunderings, an earthquake, and great hail. Then, appeared a great wonder in heaven: a woman clothed with the sun, with the moon under her feet, and upon her head a crown of twelve stars."

Revelations 11:19-12:1

FRUIT OF THE MYSTERY: TRUST IN MARY'S INTERCESSION

Pray the Our Father.
Pray ten Hail Marys.
Pray the Glory Be to the Father.
Pray the Fatima Prayer.

SEVEN SORROWS

OF MARY

SEVEN SORROWS OF MARY

Saint Bridget received this devotion from the Blessed Mother during the Middle Ages.

Devotion to the Seven Sorrows of Mary may be practiced when we wish to rid ourselves of sinful habits. This devotion consoles us as we sorrow, builds our confidence in God's mercy, protects us when temptation arises, and preserves us from relapsing into sin.

The Blessed Mother said to Saint Bridget: "No matter how numerous a person's sins may be, if one turns to me with the sincere purpose of amendment, I am prepared at once to receive such a soul graciously; for I do not regard the number of sins committed, but I look only upon the disposition with which the repentant one comes to me. I feel no aversion in healing wounds, because I am called and am in truth the Mother of Mercy."

The Seven Graces
Promised by the Blessed Mother

1. I will grant peace to the prayerful soul's family.

2. The prayerful soul will be illumined by the divine Mysteries.

3. I will console the prayerful soul in sorrow; I will help the prayerful soul serve through good works.

4. I will give the prayerful soul all that is asked for, as long as the requests do not oppose the adorable will of my divine Son or the sanctification of souls.

5. I will defend the prayerful soul in spiritual battle with the infernal enemy. I will offer protection in each moment of life.

6. I will visibly help the prayerful soul at the moment of death. Such a soul soul will see my face.

7. I have obtained this grace from my divine Son: Those who propagate this devotion to my tears and sorrows will be taken directly from this earthly life to eternal happiness, since all their sins will be forgiven. My Son and I will be their eternal consolation and joy.

COMFORT OF THE AFFLICTED

Devotion to the Seven Sorrows of Mary

A simple devotion may be offered by meditating upon each of the Seven Sorrows and praying one Hail Mary for each of them.

COMFORT OF THE AFFLICTED

How to Pray the Rosary of the Seven Sorrows of Mary

The Seven Sorrows of Mary gained new popularity following the Blessed Mother's apparitions in Kibeho, Rwanda during the 1980s. Through her apparitions, Our Lady of Kibeho asked that we pray the Rosary of the Seven Sorrows to obtain the grace of repentance. She said, "If you say the Rosary of the Seven Sorrows and meditate on it well, you will find the strength you need to repent of your sins and convert your heart. Pray my Seven Sorrows to find repentance."

INTRODUCTORY PRAYER

My God, I offer you this Rosary for your Glory, so that I can honor your Holy Mother, the Blessed Virgin, so I can share and meditate upon her suffering. I humbly beg you to give true repentance for all my sins. Give me wisdom and humility, so that I may receive all the indulgences contained in this prayer.

COMFORT OF THE AFFLICTED

Act of Contrition

O my God, I am heartily sorry for having offended you, and I detest all my sins, because I dread the loss of heaven and the pains of hell, but most of all because they offend you, my God, you who are all good and deserving of all my love. I firmly resolve, with the help of your grace, to confess my sins, to do penance, and to amend my life. Amen.

Pray Three Hail Marys

Hail Mary, full of grace, the Lord is with you. Blessed are you among women, and blessed is the fruit of your womb, Jesus. Holy Mary, Mother of God, pray for us sinners, now and at the hour of our death. Amen.

Pray the Most Merciful Mother

Most merciful Mother, remind us always about the sorrows of your Son, Jesus.

For Each of the Seven Sorrows:

COMFORT OF THE AFFLICTED

Pray the Our Father

Our Father who lives in heaven, hallowed be your name. Your kingdom come, your will be done on earth as it is in heaven. Give us this day our daily bread, and forgive us our trespasses, as we forgive those who trespass against us, and lead us not into temptation, but deliver us from evil. Amen.

Pray Seven Hail Marys

Hail Mary, full of grace, the Lord is with you. Blessed are you among women, and blessed is the fruit of your womb, Jesus. Holy Mary, Mother of God, pray for us sinners, now and at the hour of our death. Amen.

Pray the Most Merciful Mother

Most merciful Mother, remind us always about the sorrows of your Son, Jesus.

COMFORT OF THE AFFLICTED

Closing Prayer

Queen of Martyrs, your heart suffered so much. I beg you, by the merits of the tears you shed in these terrible and sorrowful times, to obtain for me and all the sinners of the world the grace of complete sincerity and repentance. Amen.

O Mary, conceived without sin, who suffered for us, pray for us.

O Mary, conceived without sin, who suffered for us, pray for us.

O Mary, conceived without sin, who suffered for us, pray for us. Amen.

COMFORT OF THE AFFLICTED

The Seven Sorrows of Mary

1. The Prophecy of Simeon

Simeon blessed them and said to Mary: "Behold, this child is destined to bring the fall and the rise of many in Israel and to be a sign, which many shall contradict; and a sword shall pierce your own soul, that the truth of many hearts may be revealed."

Luke 2:34-35

Meditation

When Mary and Joseph present the infant Jesus in the temple, Simeon foretells that the child will be sacrificed for the good of many and that Mary will suffer sorrow so deep it will pierce her soul.

2. The Flight into Egypt

After the wise men departed, behold, an angel of the Lord appeared in sleep to Joseph, saying, "Arise. Take the child and his mother, and fly into Egypt, and stay there until I shall tell you. For it will come to pass that Herod will seek the child to destroy him." Joseph arose and took the child and his mother by night, and retired into Egypt, and he remained there until the death of Herod.

Matthew 2:13-14

MEDITATION

When King Herod orders the death of all male children age two or younger, Mary and Joseph flee for safety to Egypt with the blessed infant Jesus.

3. LOSING THE CHILD

And having fulfilled the days, when they returned, the child Jesus remained in Jerusalem; and his parents knew it not. Thinking that he was in their company, they came a day's journey and sought him among their kinfolk and acquaintances. Not finding him, they returned to Jerusalem, seeking him.

Luke 2:43-45

MEDITATION

Mary and Joseph retrace their steps and search for three days, fearing that the child Jesus is lost. At last, after deep angst, they find him in the temple.

COMFORT OF THE AFFLICTED

4. THE MEETING ON THE WAY OF THE CROSS

And there followed him a great multitude of people, and a group of women who bewailed and lamented him.

Luke 43:27

MEDITATION

As Jesus makes his way to Calvary, condemned to crucifixion, he meets his mother Mary on the road. He has been flogged, humiliated, and defiled; his mother's sorrow is deep, as she watches Jesus struggle to bear his heavy cross up the hill.

5. THE CRUCIFIXION

They crucified him. By the cross of Jesus stood his mother. When Jesus had seen his mother and the disciple whom he loved standing together, he said to his mother, "Woman, behold your son." Then, he said to the disciple, "Behold your mother."

John 19:18, 25-27

COMFORT OF THE AFFLICTED

MEDITATION

Mary stands by her dying Son, sorrowfully unable to minister to him as he cries, "I thirst." She hears him promise heaven to a thief and forgive his enemies. His last words, "Behold your mother," bequeath to us Mary as our mother.

6. TAKING THE BODY DOWN FROM THE CROSS

Joseph of Arimathea, a noble counselor, went boldly to Pilate and begged for the body of Jesus. Joseph bought fine linen, and taking Jesus down from the cross, wrapped him in the cloth.

Mark 15:43-46

MEDITATION

Jesus is taken down from the cross, and his body is placed in Mary's arms. The suffering and death are finished, but for his mother, grief is only beginning. She holds the body of her Son and Lord in her arms.

7. The Burial

Near the place where he was crucified was a garden, and in the garden, a new sepulcher where no man yet had been laid. They laid Jesus there, for this was the day of preparation for the Jewish Sabbath, and the sepulcher was nearby.

John 19:41-42

Meditation

The body of Jesus is laid in the tomb. The Son no longer lives in bodily form on this earth. The long day ends with Mary alone in sorrow, awaiting the Resurrection.

LITANIES AND NOVENAS

COMFORT OF THE AFFLICTED

LITANY OF LORETO

Lord have mercy.
Lord have mercy.
Christ have mercy.
Christ have mercy.
Lord have mercy.
Lord have mercy.

Christ hear us.
Christ graciously hear us.

God our Father in heaven,
have mercy on us.
God the Son, Redeemer of the world,
have mercy on us.
God the Holy Spirit,
have mercy on us.
Holy Trinity, one God,
have mercy on us.

COMFORT OF THE AFFLICTED

Holy Mary,
> *pray for us.*

Holy Mother of God,
> *pray for us.*

Holy Virgin of virgins,
> *pray for us.*

Mother of Christ,
> *pray for us.*

Mother of the Church,
> *pray for us.*

Mother of divine grace,
> *pray for us.*

Mother most pure,
> *pray for us.*

Mother most chaste,
> *pray for us.*

Mother inviolate,
> *pray for us.*

Mother undefiled,
> *pray for us.*

Mother most amiable,
> *pray for us.*

Mother most admirable,
> *pray for us.*

Mother of good counsel,
> *pray for us.*

COMFORT OF THE AFFLICTED

Mother of our Creator,
pray for us.
Mother of our Saviour,
pray for us.
Mother of mercy,
pray for us.
Virgin most prudent,
pray for us.
Virgin most venerable,
pray for us.
Virgin most renowned,
pray for us.
Virgin most powerful,
pray for us.
Virgin most merciful,
pray for us.
Virgin most faithful,
pray for us.
Mirror of justice,
pray for us.
Seat of wisdom,
pray for us.
Cause of our joy,
pray for us.
Spiritual vessel,
pray for us.

Vessel of honor,
> *pray for us.*

Singular vessel of devotion,
> *pray for us.*

Mystical rose,
> *pray for us.*

Tower of David,
> *pray for us.*

Tower of ivory,
> *pray for us.*

House of gold,
> *pray for us.*

Ark of the covenant,
> *pray for us.*

Gate of heaven,
> *pray for us.*

Morning star,
> *pray for us.*

Health of the sick,
> *pray for us.*

Refuge of sinners,
> *pray for us.*

Comfort of the afflicted,
> *pray for us.*

Help of Christians,
> *pray for us.*

Queen of angels,
> *pray for us.*

Queen of patriarchs,
> *pray for us.*

Queen of prophets,
> *pray for us.*

Queen of apostles,
> *pray for us.*

Queen of martyrs,
> *pray for us.*

Queen of confessors,
> *pray for us.*

Queen of virgins,
> *pray for us.*

Queen of all saints,
> *pray for us.*

Queen conceived without original sin,
> *pray for us.*

Queen assumed into heaven,
> *pray for us.*

Queen of the most holy Rosary,
> *pray for us.*

Queen of families,
> *pray for us.*

Queen of peace,
> *pray for us.*

COMFORT OF THE AFFLICTED

Lamb of God, who takes away the sins of the world,
spare us, O Lord.
Lamb of God, who takes away the sins of the world,
graciously hear us, O Lord.
Lamb of God, who takes away the sins of the world,
have mercy on us.

Pray for us, O holy Mother of God,
that we may be made worthy of the promises of Christ.

Let us pray.

Grant, we beseech you, O Lord God, that we, your servants, may enjoy perpetual health of mind and body; and by the intercession of the Blessed Mary, ever Virgin, may be delivered from present sorrow, and obtain eternal joy, through Christ our Lord. Amen.

LITANY OF THE BLESSED VIRGIN MARY

Lord have mercy.
> *Lord have mercy.*

Christ have mercy.
> *Christ have mercy.*

Lord have mercy.
> *Lord have mercy.*

Christ hear us.
> *Christ graciously hear us.*

God our Father in heaven,
> *have mercy on us.*

God the Son, Redeemer of the world,
> *have mercy on us.*

God the Holy Spirit,
> *have mercy on us.*

Holy Trinity, one God,
> *have mercy on us.*

COMFORT OF THE AFFLICTED

Holy Mary,
pray for us.
Holy Mother of God,
pray for us.
Holy Virgin of virgins,
pray for us.
Chosen daughter of the Father,
pray for us.
Mother of Christ the King,
pray for us.
Glory of the Holy Spirit,
pray for us.
Virgin daughter of Zion,
pray for us.
Virgin poor and humble,
pray for us.
Virgin gentle and obedient,
pray for us.
Handmaid of the Lord,
pray for us.
Mother of the Lord,
pray for us.
Helper of the Redeemer,
pray for us.
Full of grace,
pray for us.
Fountain of beauty,
pray for us.

Model of virtue,
pray for us.
Finest fruit of the redemption,
pray for us.
Perfect disciple of Christ,
pray for us.
Untarnished image of the Church,
pray for us.
Woman transformed,
pray for us.
Woman clothed with the sun,
pray for us.
Woman crowned with stars,
pray for us.
Gentle Lady,
pray for us.
Gracious Lady,
pray for us.
Our Lady,
pray for us.
Joy of Israel,
pray for us.
Splendor of the Church,
pray for us.
Pride of the human race,
pray for us.
Advocate of peace,
pray for us.

Minister of holiness,
pray for us.
Champion of God's people,
pray for us.
Queen of love,
pray for us.
Queen of mercy,
pray for us.
Queen of peace,
pray for us.
Queen of angels,
pray for us.
Queen of patriarchs and prophets,
pray for us.
Queen of apostles and martyrs,
pray for us.
Queen of confessors and virgins,
pray for us.
Queen of all saints,
pray for us.
Queen conceived without original sin,
pray for us.
Queen assumed into heaven,
pray for us.
Queen of all the earth,
pray for us.
Queen of heaven,
pray for us.

COMFORT OF THE AFFLICTED

Queen of the universe,
pray for us.

Lamb of God, you take away the sins of the world.
Spare us, O Lord.
Lamb of God, you take away the sins of the world.
Hear us, O Lord.
Lamb of God, you take away the sins of the world.
Have mercy on us.

Pray for us, O glorious Mother of God,
that we may be made worthy of the promises of Christ.

Let us pray.
God of mercy, listen to the prayers of your servants who have honored your handmaid Mary as mother and queen. Grant that, by your grace, we may serve you and our neighbor on earth and be welcomed into your eternal kingdom, through Christ our Lord. Amen.

NOVENA TO THE BLESSED VIRGIN MARY

Opening Prayer

In the name of the Father, and of the Son, and of the Holy Spirit.
Amen.

We fly to your patronage, O holy Mother of God; despise not our petitions in our need, but deliver us always from all dangers, O glorious and blessed Virgin.

Hail, Mary, full of grace, the Lord is with you.
You have brought forth Him who made you, and remain ever a virgin.

Memorare

Remember, O most gracious Virgin Mary, never was it known that anyone who fled to your protection, implored your help, or sought your intercession, was left unaided. Inspired with this confidence, we fly to you, O Virgin of virgins and our Mother. To you do we come. Before you we stand, sinful and sorrowful. O Mother of the Word Incarnate, despise not our petitions, but in your mercy hear and answer us.

Amen.

Novena Prayer

Blessed are you among women,
and blessed is the fruit of your womb.

O pure and immaculate and likewise blessed Virgin, who is the sinless mother of your Son, the mighty Lord of the universe, you who are inviolate and altogether holy, the hope of the hopeless and sinful, we sing your praises. We bless you as full of every grace, you who bore the God-Man. We bow low before you. We invoke you and implore your aid.

Amen.

COMFORT OF THE AFFLICTED

Offer your prayerful intentions.

O Mary, conceived without sin,
pray for us who have recourse to you.

Let us pray. Holy Mary, succor the miserable, help the faint-hearted, comfort the sorrowful, pray for the people, plead for the clergy, intercede for all women consecrated to God; may all who keep your holy commemoration feel now your help and protection. Be ever ready to assist us when we pray, and bring back to us the answers to our prayers. Make it your continual care to pray for the people of God, you who, blessed by God, merited to bear the Redeemer of the world, who lives and reigns for ever and ever.
Amen.

LITANY OF THE IMMACULATE HEART OF MARY

Lord have mercy.
> *Lord have mercy.*

Christ have mercy.
> *Christ have mercy.*

Lord have mercy.
> *Lord have mercy.*

Christ hear us.
> *Christ graciously hear us.*

God our Father in heaven,
> *have mercy on us.*

God the Son, Redeemer of the world,
> *have mercy on us.*

God the Holy Spirit,
> *have mercy on us.*

Holy Trinity, one God,
> *have mercy on us.*

COMFORT OF THE AFFLICTED

Heart of Mary, after God's own heart,
pray for us.
Heart of Mary, in union with the heart of Jesus,
pray for us.
Heart of Mary, the vessel of the Holy Spirit,
pray for us.
Heart of Mary, shrine of the Trinity,
pray for us.
Heart of Mary, home of the Word,
pray for us.
Heart of Mary, immaculate in your creation,
pray for us.
Heart of Mary, flooded with grace,
pray for us.
Heart of Mary, blessed of all hearts,
pray for us.
Heart of Mary, throne of glory,
pray for us.
Heart of Mary, depths of humility,
pray for us.
Heart of Mary, victim of love,
pray for us.
Heart of Mary, nailed to the cross,
pray for us.
Heart of Mary, comfort of the afflicted,
pray for us.

COMFORT OF THE AFFLICTED

Heart of Mary, refuge of the sinner,
   pray for us.
Heart of Mary, hope of the dying,
   pray for us.
Heart of Mary, seat of mercy,
   pray for us.

Lamb of God,
you take away the sins of the world,
Lamb of God,
   spare us, O Lord.
you take away the sins of the world,
   graciously hear us, O Lord.
Lamb of God,
you take away the sins of the world,
   have mercy on us.

Christ, hear us.
   Christ, graciously hear us.

Lord, have mercy.
   Lord, have mercy.
Christ, have mercy.
   Christ, have mercy.
Lord, have mercy.
   Lord, have mercy.

COMFORT OF THE AFFLICTED

Immaculate Mary, meek and humble of heart,
    conform our hearts to the heart of Jesus.

Let us pray.

O God of infinite goodness and mercy, fill our hearts with great confidence in your most holy mother, whom we invoke as the Immaculate Heart of Mary, and grant by her most powerful intercession all the graces, spiritual and temporal, which we need, through Christ Our Lord. Amen.

NOVENA TO THE IMMACULATE HEART OF MARY

In the Name of the Father, the Son, and the Holy Spirit.
Amen.

O God, come to my assistance;
O Lord, make haste to help me.

Glory be to the Father, the Son, and the Holy Spirit.
As it was in the beginning, so it is now, and ever shall be—world without end. Amen.

Sweet Heart of Mary,
be my salvation.
Immaculate Heart of Mary,
convert sinners; save souls from hell.

Prayer to the Immaculate Heart of Mary

Immaculate Virgin, who being conceived without sin, did direct every movement of your most pure heart toward God, and was always submissive to His divine will, *obtain for me the grace to hate sin with all my heart and to learn from you to live in perfect resignation to the will of God.*

O Mary, I wonder at that profound humility, which troubled your blessed heart at the message of the Angel Gabriel that you had been chosen to be the Mother of the Son of the most high God, while you did profess yourself His lowly handmaiden.

Ashamed at the sight of my own pride, I beg of you the grace of a contrite and humble heart, so that acknowledging my misery, I may come to attain the glory promised to those who are truly humble of heart.

Blessed Virgin, who kept in your heart the precious treasure of the words of Jesus your Son, and pondering over the sublime mysteries therein contained could live only for God, I am confounded by the coldness of my heart.

Dear Mother, obtain for me the grace of meditating always on the holy law of God, and of seeking to follow your example in the fervent practice of all the Christian virtues.

O Glorious Queen of Martyrs, whose sacred heart was cruelly pierced by the sword foretold by the holy and aged Simeon in the Passion of your Son, *obtain for my heart true courage and holy patience to bear well the tribulations and trials of this wretched life; may I show myself to be your true child by crucifying my flesh and all its desires in following the mortification of the cross.*

O Mary, Mystic Rose, whose lovable heart, burning with the living fire of love, adopted us as your children at the foot of the cross, becoming thus our most tender Mother,

let me experience the sweetness of your motherly heart and the power of your intercession with Jesus in all the dangers that beset me during life, and especially at the hour of my death; in such ways may my heart be united to yours and may my heart love your Son, Our Lord, both now and through endless ages. Amen.

Atonement for Neglecting to Honor Mary

Lord, forgive all reviling of Mary's name.
We beseech you, hear us.
Lord, forgive all contempt of her Immaculate Conception.
We beseech you, hear us.
Lord, forgive all coldness in the honoring of Mary.
We beseech you, hear us.
Lord, forgive all contempt of Mary's pictures.
We beseech you, hear us.

Lord, forgive all neglect of the Holy Rosary.
We beseech you, hear us.
Lord, forgive all indifference to Mary's motherly love.
We beseech you, hear us.

An Act of Reparation

O blessed Virgin, Mother of God, look down in mercy from heaven, where you are enthroned as Queen, upon me, a miserable sinner, your unworthy servant.

Knowing full well my own unworthiness, yet in order to atone for the blasphemies, sacrileges, insults, and offenses that are done to you by the impious and blasphemous, I praise and extol you from the depths of my heart as the purest, the fairest, the holiest creature of all God's handiwork.

I bless your holy Name.
I praise your exalted privilege of being truly Mother of God, ever Virgin, conceived without stain of sin, gloriously assumed body and soul into heaven, Co-Redemptrix of the human race, and Mediatrix of all graces.

I bless the Eternal Father,
who chose you in a special way for His daughter;

COMFORT OF THE AFFLICTED

I bless the Word Incarnate,

who took upon Himself our nature in your bosom and so made you His mother;

I bless the Holy Spirit,

who took you as His bride.

All honor, praise, and thanksgiving to the ever-blessed Trinity,

who predestined you and loved you so exceedingly from all eternity as to exalt you above all creatures to the most sublime heights.

O Virgin, holy and merciful,

obtain for all who offend you the grace of repentance, and graciously accept this poor act of homage from me, your servant, obtaining likewise for me from your Divine Son the pardon and remission of all my sins. Amen.

Novena Prayer

O glorious and immaculate Heart of Mary, your soul was pierced by a sword of sorrow at the sight of the Passion of your divine Son. Intercede for me and obtain for me from Jesus…

Offer your prayerful intentions.

if it be for His honor and glory and for my good. Amen.

O heart most pure of the Blessed Virgin,
obtain for me from Jesus a pure and humble heart.

Magnificat

My soul glorifies the Lord.
My spirit rejoices in God my Savior;
for He smiles upon the humility of His servant; from this day forward, all generations will call me blessed.

The Almighty works marvels for me; holy is His name.
His mercy reaches from generation to generation, for those in awe of Him.

He puts forth His arm in strength and scatters the proud-hearted.
He casts the mighty from their thrones and raises the lowly.

He fills the hungry with good things but sends the rich away empty.
He protects His servant Israel, remembering His mercy,

the mercy promised to our fathers, to Abraham and to his descendants forever. Amen.

COMFORT OF THE AFFLICTED

Glory be to the Father, to the Son, and to the Holy Spirit.

As it was in the beginning, so it is now, and ever shall be—world without end. Amen.

In the Name of the Father, the Son, and the Holy Spirit.

Amen.

NOVENA PRAYER TO THE IMMACULATE HEART OF MARY

O Most Blessed Mother, Heart of Love, Heart of Mercy, ever listening, caring, and consoling, hear our prayer. As your children, we implore your intercession with Jesus, your Son. Receive with understanding and compassion the petitions we place before you today, especially…

Offer your prayerful intentions.

We are comforted in knowing that your heart is ever open to all who ask for your prayers. We trust to your gentle care and intercession those whom we love and who are sick or lonely or sorrowful. Holy Mother, help each of us to bear our burdens in this life, until we may share in eternal life and peace with God forever. Amen.

MIRACULOUS MEDAL NOVENA

Saint Catherine Laboure received a vision of the Miraculous Medal on November 27, 1830. In her humility, she reminds us that we ought not covet more than we are given: If we are blessed with spiritual gifts, then may we be humbly thankful, for only the Lord can one day make us worthy of such graces. If we seem to receive little or nothing, then we need not lose faith, for we realize without presumption that we are repentant sinners, no more deserving than anyone else.

St. Catherine felt clearly that, during times of sorrow, graces would be shed on we who pray with devotion. She describes her prayer life as such: "Whenever I go to the chapel, I put myself in the presence of our good Lord, and I say to Him, 'Lord, I am here. Tell me what you would have me do.' If He gives me some task, I am content, and I thank Him. If He gives me nothing, I still thank Him, since I do not deserve to receive anything more than that. And then, I tell God everything that is in my heart. I tell Him about my pains and my joys, and then I listen. If you listen, God will also speak to you, for with the good Lord, you have to both speak and listen."

Hymn

Immaculate Mary, your praises we sing.
You reign now in splendor with Jesus our king.

Ave, ave, ave, Maria!
Ave, ave, ave Maria!

In heaven the blessed your glory proclaim;
on earth we your children
invoke your sweet name.

Ave, ave, ave, Maria!
Ave, ave, ave Maria!

We pray you, O Mother, may God's will be done.
We pray for His glory; may His kingdom come.

Ave, ave, ave Maria!
Ave, ave, ave Maria!

We pray for our Mother, the Church upon earth,
and bless, holy Mary, the land of our birth.

COMFORT OF THE AFFLICTED

Ave, ave, ave Maria!
Ave, ave, ave Maria!

Opening Prayer

In the name of the Father, and of the Son, and of the Holy Spirit. Amen.

Come O Holy Spirit. Fill the hearts of your faithful, and kindle in them the fire of your love. Send forth your Spirit, and they shall be created.
And you shall renew the face of the earth.

Let us pray. O God, who instructed the hearts of the faithful by the light of the Holy Spirit, grant that by the same Spirit, we may awaken to true wisdom and rejoice in heavenly consolation, through Jesus Christ our Lord.
Amen.

O Mary, conceived without sin,
 pray for us who have recourse to you.
O Mary, conceived without sin,
 pray for us who have recourse to you.
O Mary, conceived without sin,
 pray for us who have recourse to you.

COMFORT OF THE AFFLICTED

Lord Jesus Christ, you glorified your Mother, the Blessed Virgin Mary, immaculate from the first moment of her conception. Grant that all who devoutly implore her protection on earth may eternally enjoy your presence in heaven. Lord Jesus Christ, who for the accomplishment of your greatest works have chosen the weak things of the world, that no flesh may glory in your sight, and who for a better and more widespread belief in the Immaculate Conception of your Mother have wished that the Miraculous Medal be manifested to Saint Catherine Labouré, grant, we beseech you that filled with like humility, we may glorify this mystery by word and work. Amen.

Memorare

Remember, O most gracious Virgin Mary, never was it known that anyone who fled to your protection, implored your help, or sought your intercession was left unaided. Inspired with this confidence, I fly to you, O Virgin of virgins, my mother. To you I come. Before you I stand, sinful and sorrowful. O Mother of the Word Incarnate, despise not my petitions, but in your mercy hear and answer me. Amen.

COMFORT OF THE AFFLICTED

Novena Prayer

Immaculate Virgin Mary, Mother of our Lord Jesus and our Mother, we have confidence in your powerful and never-failing intercession, manifested so often through the Miraculous Medal. We, your loving and trustful children, ask you to obtain for us the graces and favors we ask during this novena, if they be for the glory of God and the salvation of souls.

Offer your prayerful intentions.

You know, O Mary, how often our souls have been the sanctuaries of your Son who hates iniquity. Obtain for us then a deep hatred of sin and that purity of heart which will attach us to God alone, so that our every thought, word, and deed may tend to His greater glory. Obtain for us also a spirit of prayer and self-denial, that we may recover by penance what we have lost in sin and at length attain to that blessed abode where you are the Queen of Angels and of mankind. Amen.

Prayer to our Lady of the Miraculous Medal

Virgin Mother of God, Mary Immaculate, we unite ourselves to you as Our Lady of the Miraculous

Medal. May this medal be for each one of us a sure sign of your motherly affection for us and a constant reminder of our filial duties toward you. While wearing it, may we be blessed by your loving protection and preserved in the grace of your Son. Most powerful Virgin, Mother of our Savior, keep us close to you every moment of our lives, so that like you we may live and act according to the teaching and example of your Son. Obtain for us, your children, the state of grace in death, so that in union with you, we may enjoy the happiness of heaven forever. Amen.

O Mary, conceived without sin,
pray for us who have recourse to you.
O Mary, conceived without sin,
pray for us who have recourse to you.
O Mary, conceived without sin,
pray for us who have recourse to you.

Closing Prayer

O Mary, conceived without sin,
pray for us, pray for us;
O Mary, conceived without sin,
pray for us who have recourse to you.

CONSECRATIONS

AND

REPARATIONS

CONSECRATION TO THE MOST BLESSED AND SWEET VIRGIN MARY

This prayer is often attributed to St. Thomas Aquinas (1225-1274).

O MOST BLESSED and most sweet Virgin Mary, mother of God, filled with devotion, daughter of the most high king, mistress of angels, mother of all believers, today I commend to your tender heart all my deeds, my thoughts, my wishes, my desires, my speech, my activities, my whole life, and my final end; that through your prayers they may be disposed towards good, according to the will of your beloved Son, our Lord Jesus Christ; that you may be to me, O my most holy lady, helper and consoler against the wickedness and snares of the ancient enemy and against all my enemies.

From your beloved Son, our Lord Jesus Christ, graciously obtain for me the grace with which I will be able to resist the temptations of the world, the flesh, and all evil, and to always have a firm intention to sin no more. And I beg you, my most holy lady, to obtain for me true obedience and true humility of heart, that I may truly acknowledge that I am a wretched and frail sinner and powerless not only to do anything good, but also to resist the continual battles without the grace and help of my Creator and your holy prayers. Obtain for me also, O my sweetest lady, perpetual purity of mind and body, so that I may serve you and your beloved Son in your order with a pure heart and a chaste body. Obtain for me from Him a willing poverty with patience and tranquility of mind, so that I may sustain the labors of this same order and that I may work for the salvation of myself and others.

Obtain for me also, O sweetest of ladies, true charity, with which I may love your most holy Son, our Lord Jesus Christ, with all my heart, and after Him, you, above all things; and my neighbor in God and on account of God. And so I may rejoice in my neighbour's good and sorrow in his evil, and hold no one in contempt, nor judge rashly, nor exalt myself in my heart over anyone. Make me, O Queen of Heaven, to fear your Son and to equally love Him always in my heart; and of such benefits granted to me, not by my merits, but by those granted by His kindness, may I always give thanks. And of my sins, may I make a pure and sincere confession with true repentance that I may gain His mercy and grace. I pray, also, that at the end of my life, O Gate of Heaven and advocate of sinners, that you permit not your unworthy servant to deviate from the holy Catholic faith; but by your great devotion and mercy come to my aid and defend me from the evil spirits; and by the blessed and glorious passion of your Son and through your own intercession, received in hope, obtain through Him pardon from my sins. And as I die in His and your love, guide me in the way of safety and salvation. Amen.

CONSECRATION FOR VICTORY AGAINST TEMPTATIONS, ESPECIALLY THOSE OF CHASTITY

Pope Pius IX (1792-1878) advised that this be prayed morning and evening, for 100 consecutive days.

PRAY ONE HAIL MARY

Hail Mary, full of grace, the Lord is with you. Blessed are you among women, and blessed is the fruit of your womb, Jesus. Holy Mary, Mother of God, pray for us sinners, now and at the hour of our death. Amen.

O MY QUEEN! MY MOTHER! I give you all myself, and, to show my devotion to you, I consecrate to you this day my eyes, ears, mouth, heart, my entire self. Wherefore, O loving Mother, as I am your own, keep me, defend me, as your property and possession.

OFFICIAL ACT OF CONSECRATION

This prayer was written by Saint Maximillian Kolbe (1894-1941).

O IMMACULATA, Queen of Heaven and Earth, Refuge of Sinners, and our Most Loving Mother, God has willed to entrust the entire order of mercy to you. I, (*your name*), a repentant sinner, cast myself at your feet, humbly imploring you to take me with all that I am and have wholly to yourself as your possession and property. Please make of me; of all my powers of soul and body; of my whole life, death and eternity; whatever most pleases you.

If it pleases you, use all that I am and have without reserve, wholly to accomplish what was said of you: "She will crush your head," and "You alone have destroyed all heresies in the whole world." Let me be a fit instrument in your immaculate and merciful hands for introducing and increasing your glory to the maximum in all the many strayed and indifferent souls, and thus help extend as far as possible the blessed kingdom of the most Sacred Heart of Jesus. For wherever you enter, you obtain the grace of conversion and growth in holiness, since it is through your hands that all graces come to us from the most Sacred Heart of Jesus.

Allow me to praise you, O Sacred Virgin.
Give me strength against your enemies.

Amen.

ACT OF REPARATION FOR INSULTS

O BLESSED VIRGIN, Mother of God, look down in mercy from heaven, where you are enthroned as queen, upon me—a miserable sinner, your unworthy servant.

Although I know full well my own unworthiness, yet in order to atone for the blasphemies, sacrileges, insults, and offenses that are done to you by the impious and blasphemous, from the depths of my heart I praise and extol you as the purest, the fairest, the holiest creature of all God's handiwork.

ACT OF REPARATION FOR BLASPHEMY

Most glorious Virgin Mary, Mother of God and our mother, turn your eyes in pity upon us, miserable sinners. We are sore afflicted by the many evils that surround us in this life, but especially do we feel our hearts break within us upon hearing the dreadful insults and blasphemies uttered against you, O Virgin Immaculate.

O how these impious sayings offend the infinite Majesty of God and of His only-begotten Son, Jesus Christ. How they provoke His indignation and give us cause to fear the terrible effects of His vengeance.

Would that the sacrifice of our lives might avail to put an end to such outrages and blasphemies. Were it so, how gladly we should make it, for we desire, O most Holy Mother, to love and to honor you with all our hearts, since this is the will of God, and just because we love you, we will do all that is in our power to make you honored and loved by all mankind.

COMFORT OF THE AFFLICTED

In the meantime, our merciful Mother, the supreme comforter of the afflicted, accept this our act of reparation which we offer you for ourselves and for all our families, as well as for all who impiously blaspheme you, not knowing what they say. Obtain for them, from Almighty God, the grace of conversion, and so render more manifest and more glorious your kindness, your power, and your great mercy. May they join with us in proclaiming you blessed among women, the Immaculate Virgin and most compassionate Mother of God.

P̲ʀ̲ᴀ̲ʏ̲ ̲ᴛ̲ʜ̲ʀ̲ᴇ̲ᴇ̲ Hᴀɪʟ Mᴀʀʏs

Hail Mary, full of grace, the Lord is with you. Blessed are you among women, and blessed is the fruit of your womb, Jesus. Holy Mary, Mother of God, pray for us sinners, now and at the hour of our death. Amen.

ACT OF REPARATION TO THE IMMACULATE HEART OF MARY

Most Holy Virgin and our Beloved Mother, we listen with grief to the complaints of your Immaculate Heart, surrounded with thorns which the ungrateful place therein at every moment by blasphemies and ingratitude.

Moved by the ardent desire of loving you as our mother and of promoting true devotion to your Immaculate Heart, we prostrate ourselves at your feet to prove the sorrow we feel for the grief that mankind causes you and to atone, by means of our prayers and sacrifices, for the offenses with which mankind returns your tender love.

Obtain for each of us the pardon of so many sins. A word from you will obtain grace and forgiveness for us all.

Hasten, O Lady, the conversion of sinners, that they may love Jesus and cease to offend God, already so much offended, and so avoid eternal punishment.

COMFORT OF THE AFFLICTED

Turn your eyes of mercy toward us, so that, from this day forward, we may love God with all our hearts while on earth and enjoy God forever in heaven. Amen.

ACT OF REPARATION THROUGH THE BLESSED VIRGIN MARY

Mary, Virgin ever blessed! Who can worthily praise you or give thanks to you, who, by that wondrous assent of your will, did rescue a fallen world?

What honours can the weakness of our human nature pay to you, which by your intervention alone has found the way to restoration? Accept, then, such poor thanks as we crave here to offer, though they are unequal to your merits; and, receiving our vows, obtain by your prayers the remission of our offences.

Carry you our prayers within the sanctuary of the heavenly audience, and bring forth from it the medicine of our reconciliation. Through you may those sins become pardonable, the release from which we ask through you of God, and may that be granted which we demand with confidence.

Accept what we offer, grant us what we seek, spare us what we fear, for you are the sole hope of sinners. Through you, we hope for the forgiveness of our faults, and in you, most blessed Virgin, is the hope of our reward.

COMFORT OF THE AFFLICTED

Holy Mary, succour the wretched, help the faint-hearted, comfort the sorrowful, pray for the people, shield the clergy, intercede for all women consecrated to God, and let all feel your aid who keep your holy commemoration. Be you at hand, ready to aid our prayers, when we pray; and bring back to us the answers we desire. Make it your care to intercede ever for the people of God, you who, blessed of God, did merit to bear the Redeemer of the world, who lives and reigns for ever and ever. Amen.

PRAYER FOR REUNION

O Immaculate Virgin, who was preserved by a singular privilege of grace from original sin, look with pity on our separated brethren, who are still your children, and recall them to the center of unity. They have, even from afar, preserved a most tender devotion towards you, O Mother; do you, who are so generous, reward them for it by obtaining for them the grace of conversion. Victorious over the infernal serpent from the first moment of your being, now that the necessity is more urgent, renew your triumphant progress as of old. If our unhappy brethren continue in separation from our common Father, it is the work of the enemy; do you, then, unmask his wiles, put his forces to rout, and let his victims see that it is impossible to obtain salvation except in union with the successor of St. Peter. Do you, who from the first, in the plenitude of your gifts, did glorify Him who worked such great wonders in you, glorify your Son, bringing back into His one fold His strayed sheep, making them subject to the guidance of the Universal Shepherd, His Vicar on Earth; and may it be your glory, O Virgin, as well to have rooted out of the world all errors, as to have put an end to schisms, and so to have restored peace to the world.

PRAYER

O Mary, who, crowned with stars, has for a footstool under your feet, the moon, and for your throne, the wings of angels; turn your eyes upon this valley of sorrows, and listen to the voice of one who puts hope and refuge in you. You do now enjoy the infinite sweetness of paradise, but in the midst of joy and splendor, you bear always in your inmost heart the recollection of what you did suffer in this life. You have tried the needs of this exile, and therefore know how bitterly flow the days of those who live in sorrow.

Ever in your remembrance rises up a mount covered with armed men and the dregs of the people; you hear ever a voice, so well known by you, which says to you: "O Lady, behold, in my place, your son." And these thoughts move you to profound tenderness, and you do realize, O Blessed One, that on that mountain and with those words, you were destined to be the mother of the living.

Without you, what would life be to the unhappy children of Adam? Each one of them has a sorrow which tries, a grief which overwhelms, a wound which torments. And all have recourse to you, as to a port of safety, to a fount of complete refreshment. When the waves lash themselves into fury, the wayfarer turns to you and prays for calm. To you has recourse the orphan who, like a flower in the wilderness, lies exposed to the whirlwind of life. To you pray the poor who want their daily bread; and not one of them remains without help and consolation. But if all find in you aid and refreshment, what shall we say to whom you are wont to appear, glorious as you are in heaven?

O Mary, mother of all, enlighten our minds and soften our hearts, so that this most pure love which streams from your eyes may be poured forth on every side and produce those marvellous fruits, which your Son prepared for by shedding His Blood, while you did suffer the most cruel pangs at the foot of the cross.

DIVINE PRAISES

The Divine Praises traditionally follow the Benediction of the Blessed Sacrament after adoration. They may also be used as a prayer to make reparation for blasphemy and profanity.

Blessed be God.
Blessed be His Holy Name.
Blessed be Jesus Christ, true God and true Man.
Blessed be the Name of Jesus.
Blessed be His Most Sacred Heart.
Blessed be His Most Precious Blood.
Blessed be Jesus,
   in the Most Holy Sacrament of the Altar.
Blessed be the Holy Spirit, the Paraclete.
Blessed be the great Mother of God,
   Mary most Holy.
Blessed be Her Holy and Immaculate Conception.
Blessed be Her Glorious Assumption.
Blessed be the name of Mary, Virgin and Mother.
Blessed be St. Joseph, her most chaste spouse.
Blessed be God in His Angels and in His Saints.

Amen.

DEVOTIONAL PRAYERS

COMFORT OF THE AFFLICTED

PSALM 45: 9-17

The queen stands at your right hand
in the gold of Ophir.

Listen, daughter, and consider; incline your ear.
Forget your own people and your father's house;

then will the king desire your beauty.
Since he is your lord, pay homage to him.

Thus, daughter of Tyre,
the wealthiest of the people
will seek your favor with gifts.

In her chamber, the daughter of the king
is elegant indeed: Her raiment is brocade
interwoven with gold;

in embroidered robes she is led in to the king.
The virgins behind her, her bridesmaids,
are likewise brought to you.

They are led in amid joy and gladness;
they go into the royal palace.

COMFORT OF THE AFFLICTED

Your children shall take the seat of their ancestors
to serve throughout the world.

Your name will be remembered
from generation to generation.
So, people will praise you, forever and ever.

s

UNDER YOUR PROTECTION
(SUB TUUM PRAESIDIUM)

The "Sub Tuum Praesidium" is the oldest known prayer to the Blessed Mother. This verse was discovered on a piece of Greek papyrus. It dates back to approximately 300 A.D.

We turn to you for protection,
Holy Mother of God.
Listen to our prayers,
and help us in our needs.
Save us from every danger,
glorious and blessed Virgin.

COMFORT OF THE AFFLICTED

HAIL, YOU STAR OF THE OCEAN (AVE MARIS STELLA)

Star of the Ocean is one of the most ancient and widely used epithets for the Blessed Mother. It reveals her role as our hope and guiding light. This prayer is often offered for travelers. The Latin version, "Ave Maris Stella," can be traced back to the early ninth century.

Hail, you Star of Ocean!
Portal of the sky,
ever Virgin Mother
of the Lord most high.

O! by Gabriel's *Ave*,
uttered long ago,
Eva's name reversing,
establish peace below.

Break the captive's fetters;
light on blindness pour;
all our ills expelling,
every bliss implore.

COMFORT OF THE AFFLICTED

Show yourself a mother;
offer Him our sighs,
who for us Incarnate
did not you despise.

Virgin of all virgins!
To your shelter take us.
Gentlest of the gentle!
Chaste and gentle make us.

Still as on we journey,
help our weak endeavor,
'til with you and Jesus
we rejoice forever.

Through the highest heaven,
to the Almighty Three,
Father, Son, and Spirit,
one same glory be.

LOVING MOTHER OF OUR REDEEMER (ALMA REDEMPTORIS MATER)

The "Alma Redemptoris Mater," dates from the eleventh century. It is one of the four antiphons sung after Night Prayer. It is traditionally prayed during the Advent Season.

Loving Mother of the Redeemer,
Gate of Heaven, Star of the Sea,
assist your people who have fallen
yet strive to rise again.
To the wonderment of nature
you bore your Creator,
yet remained a virgin after as before.
You who received Gabriel's joyful greeting,
have pity on us poor sinners.

THE ANGEL
(ANGELUS)

The "Angelus" is a short devotional practice to honor the Incarnation. It is repeated three times daily (morning, noon, and evening) at the sound of a bell. The prayer belongs to the antiphon of Our Lady, "Alma Redemptoris." The devotion derives its name from the first word of the three versicles: Angelus Domini nuntiavit Mariae (The angel of the Lord declared unto Mary...).

The angel spoke God's message to Mary,
> *and she conceived of the Holy Spirit.*

Hail Mary, full of grace, the Lord is with you. Blessed are you among women, and blessed is the fruit of your womb, Jesus. Holy Mary, Mother of God, pray for us sinners, now and at the hour of our death. Amen.

I am the lowly servant of the Lord:
> *Let it be done to me according to your word.*

Hail Mary, full of grace, the Lord is with you. Blessed are you among women, and blessed is the fruit of your womb, Jesus. Holy Mary, Mother of

God, pray for us sinners, now and at the hour of our death. Amen.

And the Word became flesh
and lived among us.

Hail Mary, full of grace, the Lord is with you. Blessed are you among women, and blessed is the fruit of your womb, Jesus. Holy Mary, Mother of God, pray for us sinners, now and at the hour of our death. Amen.

Pray for us, holy Mother of God,
that we may be made worthy of the promises of Christ.

Let us pray. Lord, fill our hearts with your grace: Once, through the message of an angel you revealed to us the Incarnation of your Son; now, through His suffering and death, lead us to the glory of His resurrection. We ask this through Christ our Lord.
Amen.

REMEMBER (MEMORARE)

The "Memorare" first appeared as part of a fifteenth-century prayer that began "Ad sanctitatis tuae pedes, dulcissima Virgo Maria." Claude Bernard (1588-1641) popularized the idea that the Memorare was written by Saint Bernard of Clairvaux (1090-1154) of the Cistercian Order.

Remember, most loving Virgin Mary, never was it heard that anyone who turned to you for help was left unaided. Inspired by this confidence, though burdened by my sins, I run to your protection, for you are my mother. Mother of the Word of God, do not despise my words of pleading, but be merciful and hear my prayer. Amen.

HAIL QUEEN OF HEAVEN
(AVE REGINA CAELORUM)

The "Ave Regina Caelorum" is one of four antiphons sung after Night Prayer. It is traditionally prayed during the season of Lent.

Hail, Queen of Heaven;
Hail, Mistress of the Angels;
Hail, Root of Jesus;
Hail, the gate through which the light
rose over the earth. Rejoice,
Virgin most renowned
and of unsurpassed beauty,
and pray for us to Christ.

QUEEN OF HEAVEN
(REGINA CAELI)

The "Regina Caeli" is a twelfth-century antiphon for Evening Prayer sung during the Easter Season. Since the thirteenth century, it has been used as the seasonal antiphon in honor of the Blessed Virgin after Night Prayer.

Queen of Heaven, rejoice. Alleluia!
The Son whom you merited to bear, alleluia,
has risen as He said. Alleluia!
Pray to God for us. Alleluia!

Rejoice and be glad, O Virgin Mary. Alleluia!
For the Lord has truly risen. Alleluia!

HAIL, HOLY QUEEN
(SALVE, REGINA)

The "Salve, Regina" is one of four Marian antiphons sung at the end of Night Prayer, according to the season. Some believe it to have been written by Hermann the Lame (1013-1054), a monk of Reichenau. Others attribute it to Adhemar, Bishop of Le Puy, who died on August 1, 1098, though his birthdate remains unknown. The verses were also used as a processional antiphon at the Abbey of Cluny in France, c. 1135.

Hail, Holy Queen, Mother of Mercy, our life, our sweetness, and our hope. To you do we cry, poor banished children of Eve; to you do we send up our sighs, mourning, and weeping in this valley of tears. Turn, then, most gracious advocate, your eyes of mercy toward us, and after this, our exile, show unto us the blessed fruit of your womb, Jesus. O clement, O loving, O sweet Virgin Mary.

Pray for us O Holy Mother of God, that we may be made worthy of the promises of Christ. Amen.

SELECTED

LATIN PRAYERS

ROSARIUM
(THE ROSARY)

Signum Crucis (Sign of + the Cross)

In nomine Patris, et Filii, et Spiritus Sancti. Amen.

Credo (Apostles' Creed)

Credo in Deum Patrem omnipotentem, Creatorem caeli et terrae. Et in Iesum Christum, Filium eius unicum, Dominum nostrum, qui conceptus est de Spiritu Sancto, natus ex Maria Virgine, passus sub Pontio Pilato, crucifixus, mortuus, et sepultus, descendit ad inferos, tertia die resurrexit a mortuis, ascendit ad caelos, sedet ad dexteram Dei Patris omnipotentis, inde venturus est iudicare vivos et mortuos. Credo in Spiritum Sanctum, sanctam Ecclesiam catholicam, sanctorum communionem, remissionem peccatorum, carnis resurrectionem, vitam aeternam. Amen.

COMFORT OF THE AFFLICTED

Pater Noster (The Lord's Prayer)

Pater noster, qui es in caelis, sanctificetur nomen tuum. Adveniat regnum tuum, fiat voluntas tua, sicut in caelo et in terra. Panem nostrum quotidianum da nobis hodie, et dimitte nobis debita nostra sicut et nos dimittimus debitoribus nostris. Et ne nos inducas in tentationem, sed libera nos a malo. Amen.

Ave Maria (Hail Mary)

Ave Maria, gratia plena, Dominus tecum. Benedicta tu in mulieribus, et benedictus fructus ventris tui, Iesus. Sancta Maria, Mater Dei, ora pro nobis peccatoribus, nunc, et in hora mortis nostrae. Amen.

Gloria Patri (Glory Be)

Gloria Patri, et Filio, et Spiritui Sancto. Sicut erat in principio, et nunc, et semper, et in saecula saeculorum. Amen.

COMFORT OF THE AFFLICTED

ORATIO FATIMAE (FATIMA PRAYER)

Domine Iesu, dimitte nobis debita nostra, salva nos ab igne inferiori, perduc in caelum omnes animas, praesertim eas, quae misericordiae tuae maxime indigent.

SALVE REGINA (HAIL, HOLY QUEEN)

Salve Regina, Mater Misericordiae, vita, dulcedo, et spes nostra, salve. Ad te clamamus, exsules filii Hevae; ad te suspiramus gementes et flentes in hac lacrimarum valle. Eia ergo, advocata nostra, illos tuos misericordes oculos ad nos converte, et Iesum, benedictum fructum ventris tui, nobis post hoc exsilium ostende. O clemens, O pia, O dulcis Virgo Maria.

Ora pro nobis, Sancta Dei Genitrix, ut digni efficiamur promissionibus Christi.

LITANIAE LAURETANAE
(LITANY OF LORETO)

Kyrie, eleison.
> *Kyrie, eleison.*

Christe, eleison.
> *Christe, eleison.*

Kyrie, eleison.
> *Kyrie, eleison.*

Christe, audi nos.
> *Christe, exaudi nos.*

Pater de caelis, Deus,
> *miserere nobis.*

Fili, Redemptor mundi, Deus,
> *miserere nobis.*

Spiritus Sancte, Deus,
> *miserere nobis.*

Sancta Trinitas, unus Deus,
> *miserere nobis.*

COMFORT OF THE AFFLICTED

Sancta Maria,
> *ora pro nobis.*

Sancta Dei Genetrix,
> *ora pro nobis.*

Sancta Virgo virginum,
> *ora pro nobis.*

Mater Christi,
> *ora pro nobis.*

Mater divinae gratiae,
> *ora pro nobis.*

Mater purissima,
> *ora pro nobis.*

Mater castissima,
> *ora pro nobis.*

Mater inviolata,
> *ora pro nobis.*

Mater intemerata,
> *ora pro nobis.*

Mater amabilis,
> *ora pro nobis.*

Mater admirabilis,
> *ora pro nobis.*

Mater boni consilii,
> *ora pro nobis.*

Mater Creatoris,
> *ora pro nobis.*

Mater Salvatoris,
> *ora pro nobis.*

Virgo prudentissima,
ora pro nobis.
Virgo veneranda,
ora pro nobis.
Virgo praedicanda,
ora pro nobis.
Virgo potens,
ora pro nobis.
Virgo clemens,
ora pro nobis.
Virgo fidelis,
ora pro nobis.
Speculum iustitiae,
ora pro nobis.
Sedes sapientiae,
ora pro nobis.
Causa nostrae laetitiae,
ora pro nobis.
Vas spirituale,
ora pro nobis.
Vas honorabile,
ora pro nobis.
Vas insigne devotionis,
ora pro nobis.
Rosa mystica,
ora pro nobis.
Turris Davidica,
ora pro nobis.

COMFORT OF THE AFFLICTED

Turris eburnea,
> *ora pro nobis.*

Domus aurea,
> *ora pro nobis.*

Foederis arca,
> *ora pro nobis.*

Ianua caeli,
> *ora pro nobis.*

Stella matutina,
> *ora pro nobis.*

Salus infirmorum,
> *ora pro nobis.*

Refugium peccatorum,
> *ora pro nobis.*

Consolatrix afflictorum,
> *ora pro nobis.*

Auxilium Christianorum,
> *ora pro nobis.*

Regina angelorum,
> *ora pro nobis.*

Regina patriarcharum,
> *ora pro nobis.*

Regina prophetarum,
> *ora pro nobis.*

Regina apostolorum,
> *ora pro nobis.*

Regina martyrum,
> *ora pro nobis.*

COMFORT OF THE AFFLICTED

Regina confessorum,
> *ora pro nobis.*

Regina virginum,
> *ora pro nobis.*

Regina sanctorum omnium,
> *ora pro nobis.*

Regina sine labe originali concepta,
> *ora pro nobis.*

Regina in caelum assumpta,
> *ora pro nobis.*

Regina sacratissimi Rosarii,
> *ora pro nobis.*

Regina pacis,
> *ora pro nobis.*

Agnus Dei, qui tollis peccata mundi,
> *parce nobis, Domine.*

Agnus Dei, qui tollis peccata mundi,
> *exaudi nos, Domine.*

Agnus Dei, qui tollis peccata mundi,
> *miserere nobis.*

Ora pro nobis, sancta Dei Genetrix,
> *ut digni efficiamur promissionibus Christi.*

COMFORT OF THE AFFLICTED

Oremus.

Concede nos famulos tuos, quaesumus, Domine Deus, perpetua mentis et corporis sanitate gaudere; et gloriosae beatae Mariae semper Virginis intercessione, a praesenti liberari tristitia, et aeterna perfrui laetitia, per Christum Dominum nostrum. Amen.

NOVENA AD BEATAM MARIAM VIRGINEM (NOVENA TO THE BLESSED VIRGIN MARY)

In nomine Patris, et Filii, et Spiritus Sancti.
Amen.

Sub tuum praesidium confugimus, sancta Dei Genetrix; nostras deprecationes ne despicias in necessitatibus nostris, sed a periculis cunctis libera nos semper, Virgo gloriosa et benedicta.
Amen.

Ave Maria, gratia plena, Dominus tecum.
Genuisti qui te fecit, et in aeternum permanes virgo.

Memorare, O piisima Virgo Maria, non esse auditum a saeculo, quemquam ad tua currentem praesidia, tua implorantem auxilia, tua petentem suffragia esse derelicta. Nos tali animati confidentia ad te, Virgo virginum, Mater, currimus; ad te venimus; coram te gementes peccatores assistimus. Noli, Mater Verbi, verba nostra despicere, sed audi propitia et exaudi.
Amen.

Benedicta tu in mulieribus,
et benedictus fructus ventris tui.

O pura et immaculata, eadem benedicta Virgo, magni Filii tui universorum Domini Mater inculpata, integra et sacrosanctissima, desperantium atque reorum spes, te collaudamus. Tibi ut gratia plenissimae benedicimus, quae Christum genuisti Deum et Hominem: omnes coram te prosternimur: omnes te invocamus et auxilium tuum imploramus.
Amen.

Hic morare ad Beatam MariamVirginem petendam.

O Maria, sine labe concepta,
ora pro nobis qui ad te confugimus.

Oremus. Sancta Maria, succurre miseris; iuva pusillanimes; refove flebiles; ora pro populo; interveni pro clero; intercede pro devoto femineo sexu: sentiant omnes tuum iuvamen, quicumque celebrant tuam sanctam commemorationem. Assiste parata votis poscentium et reporta nobis optatum effectum. Sint tibi studia assidua orare pro populo Dei, quae meruisti, benedicta,

Redemptorem ferre mundi, qui vivit et regnat in saecula saeculorum.

Amen.

COMFORT OF THE AFFLICTED

SUB TUUM PRAESIDIUM
(UNDER YOUR PROTECTION)

Sub tuum praesidium confugimus,
Sancta Dei Genetrix.
Nostras deprecationes
ne despicias in necessitatibus,
sed a periculis cunctis libera nos semper,
Virgo gloriosa et benedicta.
Amen.

COMFORT OF THE AFFLICTED

AVE MARIS STELLA
(HAIL, STAR OF THE OCEAN)

Ave Maris Stella,
Dei Mater alma,
atque semper Virgo,
felix caeli porta.

Sumens illud *Ave*
Gabrielis ore,
funda nos in pace,
mutans Hevae nomen.

Solve vincula reis,
profer lumen caecis
mala nostra pelle,
bona cuncta posce.

Monstra te esse matrem;
sumat per te preces,
qui pro nobis natus,
tulit esse tuus.

COMFORT OF THE AFFLICTED

Virgo singularis,
inter omnes mites,
nos culpis solutos,
mites fac et castos.

Vitam praesta puram,
iter para tutum;
ut videntes Iesum
semper collaetemur.

Sit laus Deo Patri,
summo Christo decus,
Spiritui Sancto,
tribus honor unus. Amen.

ALMA REDEMPTORIS MATER
(LOVING MOTHER
OF OUR REDEEMER)

Alma Redemptoris Mater,
quae pervia Caeli Porta manes,
et Stella Maris,
succurre cadenti,
surgere qui curat, populo;
tu quae genuisti,
natura mirante,
tuum sanctum Genitorem
Virgo prius ac posterius;
Gabrielis ab ore,
sumens illud *Ave*,
peccatorum miserere.

ANGELUS
(THE ANGEL)

Angelus Domini nuntiavit Mariae,
et concepit de Spiritu Sancto.

Ave Maria, gratia plena, Dominus tecum. Benedicta tu in mulieribus, et benedictus fructus ventris tui Iesus. Sancta Maria, Mater Dei, ora pro nobis peccatoribus, nunc et in hora mortis nostrae. Amen.

Ecce ancilla Domini,
fiat mihi secundum verbum tuum.

Ave Maria, gratia plena, Dominus tecum. Benedicta tu in mulieribus, et benedictus fructus ventris tui Iesus. Sancta Maria, Mater Dei, ora pro nobis peccatoribus, nunc et in hora mortis nostrae. Amen.

Et Verbum caro factum est,
et habitavit in nobis.

COMFORT OF THE AFFLICTED

Ave Maria, gratia plena, Dominus tecum. Benedicta tu in mulieribus, et benedictus fructus ventris tui Iesus. Sancta Maria, Mater Dei, ora pro nobis peccatoribus, nunc et in hora mortis nostrae. Amen.

Ora pro nobis, sancta Dei Genetrix,
ut digni efficiamur promissionibus Christi.

Oremus. Gratiam tuam, quaesumus, Domine, mentibus nostris infunde; ut qui, Angelo nuntiante, Christi Filii tui incarnationem cognovimus, per passionem eius et crucem ad resurrectionis gloriam perducamur. Per eumdem Christum Dominum nostrum.
Amen.

MEMORARE
(REMEMBER)

Memorare, O piissima Virgo Maria, non esse auditum a saeculo, quemquam ad tua currentem praesidia, tua implorantem auxilia, tua petentem suffragia, esse derelictum. Ego tali animatus confidentia, ad te, Virgo Virginum, Mater, curro, ad te venio, coram te gemens peccator assisto. Noli, Mater Verbi, verba mea despicere; sed audi propitia et exaudi. Amen.

AVE REGINA CAELORUM
(HAIL, QUEEN OF HEAVEN)

Ave, Regina Caelorum,
ave, Domina Angelorum,
salve radix, salve porta
ex qua mundo lux est orta.

Gaude, Virgo gloriosa,
super omnes speciosa;
vale, O valde decora,
et pro nobis Christum exora.

REGINA CAELI
(QUEEN OF HEAVEN)

Regina Caeli, laetare, alleluia;
quia quem meruisti portare, alleluia,
resurrexit, sicut dixit, alleluia.
Ora pro nobis Deum, alleluia.

Gaude et laetare, Virgo Maria. Alleluia!
Quia surrexit Dominus vere. Alleluia!

SALVE REGINA
(HAIL, HOLY QUEEN)

Salve Regina, Mater Misericordiae. Vita, dulcedo, et spes nostra, salve. Ad te clamamus, exsules filii Hevae; ad te suspiramus gementes et flentes in hac lacrimarum valle. Eia ergo, advocata nostra, illos tuos misericordes oculos ad nos converte. Et Iesum, benedictum fructum ventris tui, nobis post hoc exsilium ostende. O clemens, O pia, O dulcis Virgo Maria.

Ora pro nobis, Sancta Dei Genitrix, ut digni efficiamur promissionibus Christi.

కఠోళ

CONTEMPORARY

DEVOTIONS

ఆంధ్ర

COMFORT OF THE AFFLICTED

HEAVENLY QUEEN

Heavenly Queen,
clothed with the sun,
you rise like the dawn.
 Ave Maria
Mother of Peace,
your face is the dove
of the new covenant.
 Ave Maria
Sanctum of Prayer,
your brow is clear ivory,
your heart, burnished gold.
 Ave Maria
Morning Star,
shed luminous grace
on our dark night of sin.
 Ave Maria
Mother to Saints,
bless us with wisdom
to love, serve, and pray.
 Ave Maria
Mother to Sinners,
let us obey
with love's pious devotion.
 Ave Maria

COMFORT OF THE AFFLICTED

Wellspring of Blessing,
let the flow of forgiveness
wash our hearts clear of doubt.
Ave Maria
Virgin Most Chaste,
may we live with full faith
through empty trial and sorrow.
Ave Maria
Mother of Mercy,
let no stone be cast,
as we turn from misdeed.
Ave Maria
Pillar of Flame,
may earthly temptation
burn to ash of remorse.
Ave Maria
Redeemer of Eve,
crush the head of the serpent
and the dragon, cast out.
Ave Maria
Handmaid of the Lord,
raise the downtrodden
to the light of your face.
Ave Maria

COMFORT OF THE AFFLICTED

Mother of Sorrows,
shed merciful rain
upon the drought of our sin.
   Ave Maria
Mother of Virtue,
may your blessings abundant
fill the hearts of the poor.
   Ave Maria
Most Clement Lady,
may the grace of your prayer
bring the ailing to heal.
   Ave Maria
Immaculate Heart,
let your shrine be our refuge
for now and forever.
   Ave Maria
Heavenly Queen,
you rise like the dawn
of a world without end.
   Ave Maria

COMFORT OF THE AFFLICTED

LUMINOUS PEARL

Luminous pearl
of no ocean or shell,
assumed into heaven,
crowned by the Lord,
how we lose you in sin
to the depths of despair.

Most precious heart,
chosen bride of the Lord,
may we turn from temptation,
the false promise of fool's
gold; ever to cherish
the light of your face.

Heavenly Queen,
sacred treasure untouched,
O Mother, redeem us—
small seedling pearls
cupped in the ivory
prayer of your hand.

Amen.

COMFORT OF THE AFFLICTED

ROSE OF MORNING RISING

Hail azure light of evening,
rose of morning rising;
you bring the sun's fragrance
to heal a sorrowful world.

Humble Virgin, look not upon our sins
but upon our faith, as we await
the coming of Our Lord.
Have mercy on our weakness.

In your strength, redeem us
that Our Lord's promise of salvation
be fulfilled. Eternal glory to you in the name
of the Father, the Son, and the Holy Spirit.

Amen.

COMFORT OF THE AFFLICTED

RADIANT MERCY

Mother, clothed in sun radiance,
crowned with star jewels,

bless us, wayward children
wrapped in sackcloth of sin.

We fast not with long faces,
though we yearn for your graces.

This arid day, guide us
through vast deserts of loss.

We thirst—poor in spirit
at the foot of the cross.

O Mother, sweet water,
ivory vessel of truth,

slake all worldly longing
with His wellspring of life.

Pour us out like a libation,
in the light of transfiguration.

COMFORT OF THE AFFLICTED

Renew hope beyond mourning,
the faith of souls lost,

love in this world,
His gifts often forgotten.

Forget us not in your glory;
for our hearts are contrite.

Your Son is our brother,
our feet yet made of clay.

We seek His gracious radiance
in your mercy, this day.

DEVOTIONS

Clement Mother,
lost soul that I am, I pray
receive me as an offering
at the immaculate altar
of your heart.

My deeds are unworthy,
yet let me know joy, rising
like the smoke of fragrant resin,
this heart rising within me
at each word of divine praise.

Amen.

COMFORT OF THE AFFLICTED

EVENING PRAYER

I kneel and pray
to abandon doubt,
to understand sorrow,
to trust kind intention,
to turn from temptation,
to renew sacred vow,
to believe in your heart,
and to serve the Lord daily
in each blessed soul
that thirsts for His love.

Amen.

COMFORT OF THE AFFLICTED

CHIMES

Blessed Mother,
let my heart incline
to your resonant word—

the clear ringing of bells
at dawn, noon, and dusk
calling all to pray.

COMFORT OF THE AFFLICTED

NATIVITY

Holy Virgin,
Loving Mother of God,

pray the blessed lullaby
to soothe a sorrowful heart.

Cradle souls lost to sin
in your arms of mercy.

May the weak be nourished
by the milk of your faith.

Let us each be humble
in our poverty of spirit,

friend to shepherd, king,
and gentle beast alike,

ever amazed by the wondrous star
that is the light of your face.

COMFORT OF THE AFFLICTED

GATE OF HEAVEN

Gate of Heaven,
Mother of the Redeemer,
through Our Lord's grace we serve
in a sorrowful world.

Grant that we may
    pray as you pray,
    give as you give,
    love as you love.

May we be patient with sorrow,
understanding of sin,
strong in redemption,
and steadfast in love.

May hope rise in this world
like the luminous dawn.
May we ever abide
in the radiance of your faith,

COMFORT OF THE AFFLICTED

that the Lord's will be done
here on earth as in heaven,
in the name of the Father,
the Son, and the Holy Spirit.

Amen.

www.ingramcontent.com/pod-product-compliance
Lightning Source LLC
Chambersburg PA
CBHW020000050426
42450CB00005B/261